The Knot Ultimate Wedding Planner & Organizer

The Perfect Research, Complete Worksheets, Checklists, Timelines And Budget Planning Workbook

Contents

Introduction	4
Where to Start	10
Bridal Attire	12
Beauty & Pampering	18
Bridal Registry	24
Flower Decor	32
Favors & Decor	46
Honeymoon & Accomodation	50
Invitations	56
Photography	70
Videography	76
Delegating Ceremony Duties	82
Delegating Reception Duties	86
Delegating Reception Duties	90
Who's Buying?	94
Vendor Contact & Payment Sheet	98
Reception Information	102
Sheet	102
Working Budget	106
Timeline	118
Sample Itenerary	128

Introduction

Every woman worth her salt knows that after the perfect proposal, and after showing off her sparkly new rock to cooing, admiring friends, it's almost inevitable to be assailed with a wave of uncertainty—and yes, belly-knotting panic—as she starts to wonder silently: How do I plan the wedding?

If you have ever heard the expression, "All brides are beautiful," you would be forgiven for wondering how some brides manage to be so much as passably attractive on their big day given the stress, hassles, angst, and tears that usually precede weddings. Yes, all weddings!

Tying the knot implies a permanence that in itself is vastly overwhelming and more often than not, a little bit scary—which explains why planning the wedding often seems like more of an uphill task than it actually is.

It's doubtful that any wedding in the history of the world was conducted without some measure of planning, including even flying to Vegas Britney-style at a moment's notice is its own form of planning, as impulsive as it seems. Whether you are planning a military wedding, a destination wedding, a farm wedding, a garden wedding, or even a Hawaii wedding, there are some things you don't know about preparing for one, even if you're a professional wedding planner.

Now in planning a wedding, whether as a professional wedding planner or as a bride-to-be, several factors come into play and should be considered very carefully. These include your budget, your environment, and the number of guests you could reasonably expect—taking into consideration the bride and groom's popularity and acquaintances.

Planning a wedding may very well be the hardest task any bride could ever undertake, however, it could also be the most interesting and invigorating. Especially if you have the proper guide to assist in directing your steps from the drawing room to down the aisle and ending with your honeymoon so you can start your new life with Mr. Right!

Just Engaged

How to start planning your wedding from the very day of your engagement

Getting engaged—especially after a drawn-out, tumultuous courtship—may seem like the end of a long road; but don't breathe that sigh of relief just yet because you still have the walk down the aisle to contemplate!

The very first thing you should probably do after receiving and accepting a marriage proposal is to decide on a date. At this point, it could be a tentative date or a definitive one, but both parties have to agree on the date. Listen, because men may not be very much involved in wedding planning, it is very tempting to fix a date, rent a tux, and just point them in the direction of the church. Am I right?

Well here's some advice: don't! In setting the date you absolutely must take the groom's schedule into consideration because let's face it, you wouldn't have much of a wedding to begin with if the groom is, for example, away on a missionary journey in another continent on the date you have chosen.

You should know upfront that picking a date is not the easiest thing and in fact, picking one the moment you are engaged is a definite no-no because you still have to decide on a venue and also consult the calendar of whatever venue you have chosen.

However, when it comes to a date, it certainly wouldn't hurt for you to have a general idea of what season you would like (winter, summer, autumn, spring), what major holidays you want to avoid (Thanksgiving, Christmas), etc. Oh and at this point, if you don't have a tentative timetable of all your scheduled planning activities, you are making a big mistake! You need a timetable even if you've hired a wedding planner.

Just try to be reasonable about your choice of a date because undoubtedly, having your wedding on say, Christmas morning, would be an attendance catastrophe because most of your friends and family would undoubtedly be away for the holiday.

Congratulations! You now hold the best tool for planning the wedding of your dreams. This Wedding Planner was prepared specifically for you, the very busy and well-informed bride-to-be.

The articles and worksheets were created by experinced wedding professionals, and were designed to help you plan a memorable wedding-one step at a time.

This complete guide is set out to prioritize the tasks you need to plan and organise earlier than others. We hope that you and your planner become inseparable over the coming weeks and months. Carry your planner with you as you meet with vendors and inspect locations. Feel free to photocopy worksheets as necessary for estimating and comparing your many options.

Where to Start

Before you jump headfirst into the wedding planning process, here are some helpful tips to help keep your wedding planning simple and stress free:

Do your research—look around and don't rely too heavily on just one resource

Make a list of resources you find useful and that mirror your style (our resources list right at the end of this guide is a great place to start)

Keep note of items you might need to hire as you find or think of them

Be realistic with your budget

Don't be afraid to ask for help from family and friends!

Bridal Attire

We're talking the whole shebang here. Everything from your dress and veil and your bridal party dresses to your fiancé's attire and all your accessories—it's got to fit and feel fabulous. The process of finding the perfect wedding attire for everyone begins before you even visit a salon. For your dress, start pulling pictures from magazines of dresses you like to take with you when you visit the salon or seamstress.

For your bridal party, keep in mind their various body types, coloring, personalities, and financial constraints. For the guys, this is often where your fiancé has a strong opinion, so be open to his input and let him find what he wants to wear—you've got enough to worry about! As for your accessories, they are a necessity and part of your overall wedding day attire. Finding the right jewelry, veil, headpiece, hairpiece, shoes, or bag shouldn't be an afterthought.

Put some thought into this even as you're purchasing your dress and other bridal attire, and you'll have an easier time pulling your ensemble together to create the image you've been dreaming about since you were a little girl.

Tips and To-Dos

Show And Tell: Bring your tear sheets of gowns with you and offer them to the consultants at the salon. This will give them a good starting point and you can begin narrowing down styles you like to the ones that fit and flatter you most.

That's What Friends Are For: Bring someone you trust with you to shop. You need a second (or third or fourth) opinion sometimes to help you decipher what styles, fabrics, and colors suit you best.

The Dress You've Been Waiting For: Wait at least a day before you buy the dress you think you want. Think about it. Discuss it with whoever shopped with you and some other friends or family. If you still think it's the dress the next day, go back, try it on again, and then make your decision. This will ensure you've thought it through and are shopping and acting rationally.

Sew Perfect: The perfect dress doesn't have to cost a fortune. And if it does, and you're on a budget, take a picture of it to a reputable seamstress and see if she can recreate it for a fraction of the price. If money is no object then ignore this tip and call me—I'd love to plan your wedding!

Be Nice: Offer your bridesmaids some options other than the standard cookie-cutter bridesmaid's dress. Shop off the rack, give them a color, style and/or designer and let them choose, and be sensitive about costs.

What A Guy Wants: Since the bride usually has so much input in the overall wedding, it's important that in areas that really matter to your fiancé to let him have his say and yes—his way! Talk about some parameters of his attire (formality, color scheme, etc.) and then let him be. If he doesn't care what he wears, then by all means, have at it!

Bridal Attire Worksheet

Bridal Gown

Bridal Shop: _____

Contact person: Phone: Fax:
Address:
Website: E-mail address:

Designer/Manufacturer: Style:
Color/Fabric: Train Length:
Size: Cost:

Designer/Manufacturer: Style:
Color/Fabric: Train Length:
Size: Cost:

Fitting Date: _____

First Fitting (date/time):   Second Fitting (date/time):
Final Fitting (date/time):   Pick-up (date/time):
Cost: Cost:

Head Piece/Veil: _____

Style: Color:
Length: Cost:

Bridesmaids Attire

Contact person:　　　　Phone:　　　　Fax:
Address:
Website:　　　　　　　E-mail address:

Company: _____

Designer/Manifacture:　　　Style:
Color/Fabric:　　　　　　　Size:　　　　Cost:
Accessories:

Alterations Contact:　　　Phone:　　　　Fax:
Alteration Specifications:

Fitting Date: _____

First Fitting (date/time):　　Second Fitting (date/time):
Final Fitting (date/time):　　Pick-up (date/time):
Cost:　　　　　　　　　　　Cost:

Flower Girl Dress: _____

Designer/Manifacture:　　　Style:
Color/Fabric:　　　　　　　Size:　　　　Cost:
Accessories:

I'm a firm believer in the whole "look good, feel good" philosophy, and looking good is never more important than on your wedding day. Getting the right person or persons to do your hair and/or makeup is key.

But looking good and feeling good for your wedding day is actually a process that can begin days or weeks before your big day. Some brides will schedule spa days, facials, nail appointments, and massages to help them unwind and prepare.

Every woman is different and you need to find what relaxes and rejuvenates you, and go for it.

Tips and To-Dos

Plan Ahead: It's never too early to start thumbing through magazines and pulling makeup and hairstyles you like. Bring those tear sheets with you to your practice session along with your veil, tiara, and any other accessories you're planning to wear. It's a good idea to bring a picture of your dress, since often the style of your dress can dictate what hairstyles will look good.

Ask Around: Ask for references from past clients and call the references. You can also ask to see photos from past weddings they've done before you book them.

Look Your Best: ALWAYS get a consultation with your potential stylist/makeup artist. This will help you both to get an idea of exactly what you want. You will probably have to pay for it, but it's worth it. Most will charge you less for the consult than the actual job itself.

Leave It To The Pros: Many brides aren't used to wearing a lot of makeup on a daily basis. Keep in mind that a good professional makeup artist has an eye for "how much is too much." Let them know ahead of time that you want a very natural look and let them do their magic. Take pictures at your consultation so you both can see how the makeup

comes out in pictures.

Get With The Times: If you have multiple people getting their hair and/or makeup done, work with your stylist/makeup artist to create a timeline of approximately how long each person will take and what time they should be there, ready to get-ready. Then tell those getting their hair/makeup done to be there at least thirty minutes earlier than they are scheduled in case the timeline varies a little.

Show Them The Money: Find out exactly what the terms of payment are. Most often you have to pay them by cash or cashier's check.

Hair: _ _ _ _ _ _ _ _ _ _ _ _

Salon/company: Appointment with:
Phone: Fax:
Consultant(date/time):   Wedding Day App.(date/time):
Address:
Website: Email Address:
Deposit Ammount:
Total Cost of Services Provided:

Make Up: _ _ _ _ _ _ _ _ _ _ _

Salon/company: Appointment with:
Phone: Fax:
Consultant(date/time):   Wedding Day App.(date/time):
Address:
Website: Email Address:
Deposit Ammount:
Total Cost of Services Provided:

Nails: _ _ _ _ _ _ _ _ _ _ _

Salon/company: Appointment with:
Phone: Fax:
Consultant(date/time):   Wedding Day App.(date/time):
Address:
Website: Email Address:
Desired service:
Total Cost of Services Provided:

Spa:_____

Salon/company: Appointment with:
Phone: Fax:
Consultant(date/time): Wedding Day App.(date/time):
Address:
Website: Email Address:
Desired service:

Total Cost of Services Provided:

Bridal Registry

Registering can be fun but only if you're prepared! Some couples view this as an unnecessary ritual that can take them hours with little benefit or purpose. Wrong, wrong, wrong! Do yourself, and your guests, a favor and take the time it takes to register.

It allows your guests to get you something you actually want and need; it cuts down on the time you'll spend returning unwanted gifts later.

So clear your calendar, give yourself a few hours with your fiancé, and go shopping! It's one of the few times you'll be allowed such an elaborate shopping list—*and it won't cost you a thing!*

Tips and To-Dos

Where in the world? Register at a place or places where guests can access your registry, in person or online. Make it easy on those buying your wedding gifts to find what you want. If you have a lot of mainland guests attending, try to register at a place that is accessible to everyone (i.e.: Macys, Neiman Marcus, Pier One, etc.)

The Time Is Now: Register at any time before the invites go out. But a good time to do it is five to eight months prior to your wedding date. That is one less thing you'll have to worry about closer to your wedding, and you can always make changes after your initial registry.

Just What You Asked For: It's acceptable and okay nowadays to register for almost anything that your bridal registry store carries. That's why registering in department stores (Sears, JC Penney) or discount superstores (Target, Walmart, etc.) is popular with couples.

It's A Gift: After you've completed your registry, go to that same store at a different location or to that same store the next day, to make sure that everything on your registry was processed correctly and that it is easy to access and understand. Don't make gift-giving difficult for your guests.

Checking In: Check back periodically with your registry to see if you need to add items or change anything.

Too Much Of A Good Thing: It's okay to register at multiple stores, but don't get carried away. Two stores is a good number, too many more and you're spreading yourself thin and narrowing the odds that people are going to go hunting for what you want. Sometimes too many options can be a bad thing.

Caterers Worksheet

Careter: _____

Company: Contact Name:
Phone: Fax:
Address:
Website: Email Address:

Type of service: _____

- Bufiet   Sit Down   Pupus   Cake&Punch
- Other
- Specialy Foods/Service

Menu Selection: _____

Services: _____

Kitchen Facilities:	Cost:
Food Prep&Equipment:	Cost:
Servers Provided:	Cost:
Bartenders Provided:	Cost:
Gratuity Included?	Cost:
Beverage Services:	Cost:
Set-up:	Cost:
Clean-up:	Cost:
Cake:	Cost:

Cake Knife Set & Supplies:	Cost:
Linens/Napkins:	Cost:
Ice Carvings:	Cost:
Other:	Cost:
Other:	Cost:

Cost:_____

Per Person:	Estimated Guests:
Total Cost:	
Menu Selection Due Date:	
Final Head Count Due Date:	
Deposit Due Date:	Deposit Amount:
$	Balance Due on:

Consultant Worksheet

Consultant: _____

Company: Contact Name:
Phone: Fax:
Address:
Website: Email Address:

Services: _____

Reception Location	Flowers
Reception Coordination	Cake/Baker
Ceremony Location	Party/Equipment Rental
Ceremony Coordination	Favors/Decorations
Bridal Gown Rentals & Sales	Invitations/Stationary
Custom Sewing & Alterations	Bridal Registry
Bridesmaid Dresses	Entertainment/Music
Formal Wear	Transportation
Caterer	Honeymoon
Beverage Service	Jewelry
Photographer	Attendant Gifts
Videographer	Rehearsal
Beauty	Rehearsal Dinner
Other	
Other	
Other	

Terms of payment (Select One) : _____

Flat Fee Based on Services Agreed Upon:
Hourly:
Percentage (of budget):
Deposit Due Date: Deposit Amount:
$ Balance Due on:

Be sure to have your terms of agreement contract with your wedding planner attached to this worksheet. It should have a detailed account of all services provided and costs.

The flowers you use to enhance the ambience of your wedding and ceremony can transform even the most mundane location into a stunning backdrop. Never underestimate the power of beautiful flowers, or better yet, a talented florist. This is one budget line item that can vary in extremes depending on what florist you book.

Nowadays many florists work with actual designers who can create elaborate arrangements, backdrops, centerpieces—whatever your heart desires—if you're willing and able to pay for it. Set your budget; start clipping ideas and set at least two or three appointments with prospective florists.

Tips and To-Dos

Shop Around: I always recommend you meet with several vendors in each category before booking one, and your florist is no exception. You want to book someone you have a good rapport with and who seems to really grasp the look and feel you're going for. Be open to their ideas and suggestions. In the end, it will be the value of their expertise that you are paying for, not just some pretty flowers.

Go Prepared: Before appointments with your prospective florists, be sure to have the following information: time and location of your ceremony and/or reception, any restrictions for flowers your sites may have, color scheme and theme of your wedding, a picture of your gown, pictures or swatches of bridesmaids dresses, and photos of flower arrangements that you like. This will save you and your florists a lot of time and will help both of you decide what will work best.

By Appointment Only: If the florist is available, schedule an appointment and ask if they charge a consulting fee. Plan to meet with the florist for about an hour. This will give you enough time to look through their portfolios, see some samples, and ask lots of questions.

Aisle Do It My Way: Lining the aisles with loose flowers is an inexpensive way to add color and charm to a ceremony, especially for outdoor weddings.

Double Duty: Use the arrangements and other pieces from the ceremony site for decor at the reception site. If you don't have a full-service florist do your wedding, assign the duty to someone else.

Ceremony Flowers Worksheet

Florist: _____

Company:	Contact Name:
Phone:	Fax:
Address:	
Website:	Email Address:

Delivery: _____

Ceremony Location:
Date:	Time:

Ceremony Flowers	Quantity	Cost Per	Total
Bridal Bouquet/Flowers:			
Bridal Throw:			
Headpiece/Haku:			
Bridesmaids Bouquet/Flowers:			
Bridesmaids Headpiece/Haku:			
Flower Girl's Basket:			
Flower Girl's Headpiece/Haku:			

Mother-of-the-Bride Corsage:			
Mother-of-the-Groom Corsage:			
Father's Boutonniere/Lei:			
Groom's Boutonniere/Lei:			
Groomsmen's Boutonniere/Lei:			
Usher's Boutonniere/Lei:			
Ringbearer's Boutonniere/Lei:			
Step Parent's Corsage/Boutonniere/Lei:			
Grandparent's Corsage/Boutonniere/Lei:			
Parent's Thank You Bouquets/Leis:			

Special Guests s/leis	Quantity	Cost Per	Total
Out of Town Guests:			
Emcee/Entertainment:			
Guest Table Attendant:			
Officiant:			
Wedding Planner:			
Ceremony Decor:			
Lattice/Archway:			
Aisle:			
Altar Arrangements:			
Pew Arrangements:			
Communion Table:			
Unity Candle:			
Candelabra Arrangements:			
Chairs:			
Other:			

Florist: _____

Company:	Contact Name:
Phone:	Fax:
Address:	
Website:	Email Address:

Delivery: _____

Ceremony Location:
Date: Time:

Reception Flowers	Quantity	Cost Per	Total
Head Table:			
Family Table:			
Buffet Table:			
Cake Table:			
Guest Table:			
Centerpiece Arrangements			
Favors:			
Podium:			
Other:			

Centerpieces: _____

Supply Store: Cost:
Phone: Fax:
Address:
Website: Email address:
Supplies Needed:

Favors: _____

Supply Store: Cost:
Phone: Fax:
Address:
Website: Email address:
Supplies Needed:

Other Decorations & Misc. Supplies: _____

Equipment Rental Worksheet

Rental: _____

Company:	Contact Name:
Phone:	Fax:
Address:	
Website:	Email Address:

Delivery: _____

Ceremony Location:
Date: Time:

Wedding Items	Quatity	Cost
Aisle Runner:		
Arches:		
Buffet Table:		
Cake Table:		
Candelabra:		
Chairs:		
Chairs Covers:		
Dance Floor:		
Flower Stands:		
Gazebos:		
Hurricane Lamps:		
Kneeling Benches:		

Pillars:		
Round Tables:		
Stanchions:		
Table Mirrors:		
Tens/Canories:		
Other:		
Other:		
Beverage Item		
Bar:		
Beer Taps&Kegs:		
Beverage Fountains:		
Champagne Buckets:		
Coffee Makers:		
Coolers:		
Other:		
Others:		
Flower Stands:		
Gazebos:		

Linens	Quatity	Cost
Napkins Color:		
Buffet Table Covers: Color: Size:		
Round Table Covers: Color: Size:		
Cake Table Covers: Color: Size:		

Service/Flatware: _____

Cake Knife Set:		
Coffee&Tea Service:		
Punchbowl:		
Punchbowl Glasses:		
Serving Utensils:		
Trays:		
China:		
Flatware:		
Glassware:		

Miscellaneous rental: _____

Balloon&Helium Tank:		
Lavaliere:		
Podium:		
Sound System:		

Standing Mie:		
Lighting:		
Other:		
Other:		
Subtotal		
Total		
Tax		

Rehearsal Dinner Information

This day is important for several reasons. It gives you a chance to do a dry run and get out any kinks in your ceremony timeline. It's important that you invite key people involved in your ceremony. It also serves as a nice time to thank family and friends who have been an important part in your wedding planning and in your lives and introduce family who may not have already.

Ceremony Rehearsal:_____

Size:
Date: Time:
Contact: Phone: Fax:
Address:
Website: Email Address:
Parking Info:
Confirmed Rehearsal Site/Date/Time: Yes   No
Number of People Attending:
Total Cost:

Dinner:_____

Size:
Date: Time:
Contact: Phone: Fax:
Address:
Website: Email Address:
Parking Info:
Confirmed Rehearsal Site/Date/Time: Yes   No
Number of People Attending:
Total Cost:

Guest List: Be sure to include officiant, bridal party, flower girl, ring bearer, musicians (if necessary), family, friends, special guests.

Guests	RSVP	Guests	RSVP

Favors & Decor

How you choose to tie your theme together is most often reflective in the types of favors, centerpieces, and overall decor.

Some couples (usually the women) get totally into this part of the wedding planning. If you're creative you can find hundreds of ways to add special touches to your ceremony and reception. And if you're not creative, you can do what many of us do, and "borrow" ideas from magazines, books, and online.

There are many companies who specialize in creating just the right pieces to make your wedding day extra special.

Tips and To-Dos

Do Me A Favor: Many brides enlist the help of girlfriends to help tie, fold, cut, clip, and create "Martha-esque" favors and décor—a good idea if you have some time to spare and lots of willing and able friends. This can backfire if you have hundreds of favors to do with limited knowledge, resources, or help. Get a quote from companies that specialize in these before you try taking on this sometimes overwhelming task yourself. It may just be worth letting a professional handle.

You've Come A Long Way Baby: Gone are the days where a lone chocolate kiss serves as a wedding favor. Now you can find personalized candy bars, chopsticks, custom made CDs, photo keepsakes, elaborate handmade trinkets, and so much more. All of these are wonderful but they can get costly. If you're looking at ways to cut your wedding budget and have elaborate favors and centerpieces included in your budget, you may want to consider cutting back. This is one area where guests will appreciate whatever they get and you don't have to go into debt giving them something fancy and expensive.

Favors Worksheet

Favors: _____

Company: Contact Name:
Phone: Fax:
Address:
Website: Email Address:
List favors and quantities:

Total: Deposit Paid: Date:
Balance Due: Balance Due Date:

Decorations: _____

Company: Contact Name:
Phone: Fax:
Address:
Website: Email Address:
List specific items (i.e. balloons, backdrops, table decorations, etc.) and quantities:

Total: Deposit Paid: Date:
Balance Due: Balance Due Date:

Old-school traditions have the man planning and paying for the honeymoon, but as with many traditions, this one is open for interpretation and anything goes! If you're planning a destination wedding, chances are it's serving as both your wedding ceremony and honeymoon site—so plan accordingly!

Tips and To-Dos

Book 'Em Dano! One of the easiest and often least expensive ways to book your honeymoon and accommodations is through a travel agent or tour operator. It's a one-stop shop for all your travel needs. You can almost always book your air, room, and car through the travel agent. Check online or in the Sunday paper for discounts on travel packages.

Stick To Your Budget: Include your honeymoon and accommodations into your wedding budget. Many couples don't include this expense and don't realize until it's too late what a costly line item this can be. Make sure you think about all costs you're likely to incur including extras like service charges, tips, souvenirs, and shopping sprees. If you are planning to honeymoon overseas, keep an eye on exchange rates; any major fluctuations can affect your budget.

Your Walking Papers: With heightened security at airports around the world, you have to be prepared with all the necessary travel documents. Make sure you have current identification, passports, credit cards, and other necessary documents to travel. If you're not sure what you need, ask your travel agent. You will want to purchase your airline ticket using your maiden name because your photo ID needs to match the name on the ticket.

Fly Bye: If at all possible, plan to leave for your honeymoon a day or two after your wedding. Most couples are exhausted by the time their wedding is over and trying to get on a plane that same day can add unnecessary stress. Give yourself some time to enjoy each other, pack,

and properly prepare for your honeymoon.

A Friend In The Business: Whether you're going around the corner or around the world, be sure to find a good travel agent that you can talk to and ask lots of questions.

Gettin' The Hook Up: Inform the resort, hotel, or bed & breakfast that this is your honeymoon. They may surprise you with special accommodations: room upgrade, complimentary wine, or something special to help you celebrate.

Honeymoon Worksheet

Destination: _____

Location: Date Booked:
Travel Agent Name: Phone: Fax:
Confirmation Numbers:
Date of Departure: Date of Return:
Departing From: Arriving At:
Layovers/Connecting Flights:
Departure Flight Number: Airline:
Return Flight Number: Airline:

Hotel/Ship: _____

Name: Phone:

Car rental: _____

Agency: Phone:
Confirmation Number:
Pickup (date/time):   Return (date/time):

Insurance information (travel, baggage, car, etc.): _____

Travel Requirements/Paperwork/Documents: _____

Cost (including tax, service, and port charges): _____

Total:
Deposit Paid: Date:
Balance Due: Due Date:
Allocated Spending Money (for shopping, food, entertainment, etc.):

Total honeymoon budget: _____

Your invitations should be in line with your wedding theme and the formality of your wedding. They are your guests' first impression of your wedding. Wedding invitations can be expensive, but you don't have to spend an excessive amount of money to convey the style and formality of your special day.

There are several elements you should consider when selecting your invitations or shopping around to make your own invitations.

Look at the weight of the paper, the shade, font style and size, size of invitations and envelopes, wording, general style, and postage restrictions and costs.

Tips and To-Dos

Guest Who? Before you mail off your invitations, number the backs of the response cards and keep a master list. Sometimes guests will forget to write their names on the response cards. If they are pre-numbered, you can compare the number on the back to the names on your master list and find out who the guest is.

Same Old, Same Old: If possible, use the same kind of stationery for everything. Order everything at one time and order more than you think you need. If you're making your own invitations, order extra paper, velum, envelopes, and anything else you need to create them. It's less expensive to order extra the first time than to have to make a small reorder because you don't have enough. Place invitation orders four to six months out.

It's In The Mail: Mail invitations six to eight weeks before your wedding and be sure to include, on your reply card, an RSVP deadline of two to three weeks before the wedding. This will give you time to inform the reception site and caterer of how many to expect and to make any last minute phone calls to guests who may not have replied.

Crack The Code: When addressing envelopes, double-check the zip

code! If you're not sure, use these websites as a reference: www.usps.gov (in the US) www.canadapost.ca (in Canada)

Made-to-Order: Decide what you will be ordering and including with your invitation. There is no "wrong" or "right," but typically most brides order invitations, inner and outer envelopes, reception cards, response cards, and response card envelopes.

The Write Way: Address all envelopes by hand. Write neatly. If your handwriting isn't acceptable, recruit some family or friends with nice penmanship. You can also opt to have your envelopes addressed by a calligrapher. Have the correct spelling of absolutely everything. Spell out names and numbers in full. Do not abbreviate except for Mr., Mrs., Ms., or Dr. Print the guest's full name on the outside envelope (i.e. Mr. and Mrs. Mel DeLaura). The inside envelope only needs to have their last name (i.e. Mr. and Mrs. DeLaura).

Invitations Worksheet

Stationery: _____

Store/Stationer:
Contact: Phone: Fax:
Address:
Website: Email Address:

Invitations: _____

Style or Item Number: Paper Color:
Lettering Style/Font: Ink Color:
Quantity Ordered: Price:

Text for Invitation (Consult your stationer for wording examples): _____

Line 1	
Line 2	
Line 3	
Line 4	
Line 5	
Line 6	
Line 7	
Line 8	
Line 9	
Line 10	
Line 11	

Line 12	
Line 13	
Line 14	
Line 15	
Line 16	

Outer envelope:_____

Style or Item Number: Envelope Color:
Lettering Style/Font: Ink Color:
Lining Color:
Quantity Ordered: Price:

Text for outer envelope:_____

Line 1	
Line 2	
Line 3	
Line 4	

Worksheet Invitations

Inner envelope (no printing required) :_____

Style or Item Number: Envelope Color:
Quantity Ordered: Price:

Text for reception card :_____

Line 1	
Line 2	
Line 3	
Line 4	

Thank you notes :_____

Style or Item Number: Paper Color:
Lettering Style/Font: Ink Color:
Quantity Ordered: Price:

Text for thank you notes :_____

Line 1	
Line 2	
Line 3	
Line 4	

Place cards: (pre printing is optional):_____

Style or Item Number: Paper Color:
Lettering Style/Font: Ink Color:
Quantity Ordered: Price:

Text for place cards:_____	
Line 1	
Line 2	
Line 3	
Line 4	

Think about how you are going to arrive at your ceremony and/or reception site. Unless you're on an extremely tight budget, hiring a limousine service is relatively inexpensive and it does add some class and an air of something special to your wedding day.

There are several benefits to renting a limo or special transportation. You don't have to worry about parking or designating a driver to get you to and from your ceremony and reception.

You can transport your entire bridal party, if necessary, to ensure that you are all where you need to be when you need to be there. Although white stretch limousines are the norm for weddings, other types of vehicles (Rolls-Royce, PT Cruisers, Stretch SUVs, sports cars, and even trolleys) are available for rent. Begin looking for your transportation company two to three months before your wedding. If you plan to rent specialized vehicles, you may want to book your transportation earlier because vehicles of this type are popular.

Tips and To-Dos

You're Better Off: Before you book your transportation, call the Better Business Bureau. The most common complaint lodged against transportation companies is a "no-show" or "late-show" complaint. Disreputable transportation companies will often overbook themselves or will forgo a wedding booking for a more profitable one. There are no guarantees, but checking with the BBB will help you weed out those that have a reputation for inconsistency. Another way to avoid this is to book a transportation company that specializes in weddings.

Only A Phone call Away: Call and do phone interviews with several transportation companies. Schedule a day to inspect the operation and vehicles you're interested in from the top few companies you've narrowed down.

Prefer The Referred: Have your top two preferences give you reference names and numbers of couples who have recently used their transportation services for their own wedding. You can also get references of good transportation companies from your other wedding vendors (photographers, wedding planners, etc.)

Living Large: Consider the size of your passengers, your wedding gown, and other things you may be travelling with when booking your transportation. Limos and other specialized vehicles come in various sizes (six-passenger, eight-passenger, ten-passenger, etc.) Make sure your vehicle is large enough to comfortably accommodate your needs.

On A First Name Basis: Get the name and contact number of the driver or dispatch person directly involved with your booking in case of any last minute changes or emergencies.

Transportation Wedding Day

Transportation: _____

Company: Contact Name
Phone: Fax:
Address:
Website: Email Address:
Cost per Hour   Minimum Hours: Overtime Rate:
Type of Vehicle(s):

To ceremony site: _____

Name	Pick-up Time	Pick-up Location	Driver's Name/Number
Bride & Groom			
Bridesmaids			
Groomsmen			
Bride's Parents			
Groom's Parents			
Other Guests			
Other Guests			

From ceremony site: _____

Name	Pick-up Time	Pick-up Location	Driver's Name/Number
Bride & Groom			
Bridesmaids			
Groomsmen			
Bride's Parents			

Groom's Parents			
Other Guests			
Other Guests			

There are dozens and dozens of good wedding photographers to choose from. For many, this is one of the most expensive and difficult decisions to make, in part because of all the options out there.

The best way to start looking for a wedding photographer is to visit the expos, get online and check out their websites, and find the photographers whose style you like best.

Meet with a few and you should have no problem finding the right one for you. Some specialize in black and white photographs; some have the latest and greatest digital capabilities; others devote the entire day with you, capturing every moment.

Tips and To-Dos

Charmed I'm Sure: Book a photographer that you like. Personality matters and you need to be sure you "click" and that you can handle spending the most important day of your life with this person as he/she tells you where to stand, when to smile, and what to do. Meet with at least two photographers before booking, but don't wait too long once you find one you like. The good photographers tend to book quickly.

Read The Fine Print: Ask about hidden costs or additional charges (travel fees, extra film, enlargements, extra cost for black and white photos, etc.) Ask if negatives are included in the package or if they are available for purchase.

Timing Is Everything: Discuss your wedding timeline and any special events you want to ensure that your photographer covers. Be sure to give them a wedding day itinerary. This will give them a written schedule to follow and will make sure they know what to expect and when to expect it. Be sure to include the moments, people, and things you particularly want captured in your wedding photographs.

All In The Family: Assign a friend or family member to help the photographer round up people who are to be in the formal pictures. It may be necessary to have two people, one for the groom's family and one for the bride's. In addition, let those who are expected to be in the formal photos know ahead of time and ask them to be at a specific location immediately following the ceremony.

Let's Be Candid: If you're looking for ways to save money, have a photographer shoot the ceremony and formals and have friends and family take candid photos at the reception.

Write On! Don't settle for an oral agreement. Get all the terms in writing and make sure both parties sign the contract as soon as you book the date. Read the entire contract (fine print included!). As with all your vendors, check with the Better Business Bureau to see if they are members and/or if they have had any complaints against them. The Chamber of Commerce is another good resource for checking potential vendors. Better yet, ask brides recently married for their recommendations.

Photographers Worksheet

Studio Information: _____

Studio: Photographer's Name
Phone: Fax:
Address:
Website: Email Address:
Assistant's Name Phone:

Services needed: _____

- Rehearsal   Pre-Ceremony   Ceremony   Reception
- Other:

Report time/location: _____

Rehearsal
Pre-Ceremony
Ceremony

Package included (Number of proofs, enlargements, touch-ups, negatives number of hours, travel fee, albums, cost for additional prints, etc):

Photo ready dates :_____

Proofs:
Final Prints:
Photo Album(s):

Total package :_____

Cost:
Deposit Paid: Date:
Balance Due: Due Date:

Make sure you attach your signed contract with all the stipulations, specifics, and terms of agreement to this worksheet. Be sure to review the tips and questions to ask carefully before signing a contract.

Couples are opting to include a video as a part of their reception program. Today's technology allows videographers to edit in photos, special video clips, and music along with video excerpts of wedding day prep, photos, the ceremony, and more.

A well-done wedding video can tell the couple's love story, capture their fondest memories, and share some of their favorite moments. It's a good way to have the guests get to know the bride and/or groom; it serves as a nice addition to your reception program.

Many couples opt to spend less on a photographer and more on a high-quality wedding video that they can easily preserve, duplicate, and watch for years to come.

Tips and To-Dos

Ample Samples: If you want to book a videographer, ask to see some actual wedding videos shot by the person who will be doing your recording. Make sure the person who is shooting your wedding is the one you meet with and whose work you have seen. You don't have to watch the entire video of course, but if you only watch the demos they choose to show you, be aware that you are watching their best work. Watch and note how the videos flow. Ask lots of questions and make notes of things you like and don't like.

Perfect Timing: One of the first questions couples ask is how long should a wedding video/movie be. You'll find they range from thirty minutes to three hours and everything in between. There is no wrong or right answer, but it seems like the happy medium is between an hour to an hour and a half.

Get To The Specifics: Get a written agreement of exactly what type of video coverage you want: number of cameras and videographers, type of editing, music, special graphics and effects, names of camera persons and editors, the date, time, and location of the ceremony. Most responsible companies will require a deposit. Some companies will want to be paid fully in advance and others will have some kind of payment schedule.

Going Hollywood: There are many different video formats in use today, but the ones most commonly used by wedding videographers are VHS, S-VHS, and DV. The quality of the DV (digital video) is far superior to VHS and S-VHS. Opt to have your wedding captured with DV and delivered to you on DVD, if at all possible.

Show Off: Some companies, as an option, will start your video with a section containing the bride's and groom's childhood pictures, then dating pictures, some photos with family and friends, and they will edit in footage from your ceremony.

Videographers Worksheet

Video Information: _____

Company:	Videographer's Name
Phone:	Fax:
Address:	
Website:	Email Address:
Assistant's Name	Phone:

Services needed: _____

Rehearsal   Pre-Ceremony   Ceremony   Reception
Other:

Report time/location: _____

Rehearsal
Pre-Ceremony
Ceremony
Reception

Package included (Number of video tapes, number of hours, video tape length, turn arround time for slide show video, cost for additional tapes, etc):

Total package : _____

Cost:
Deposit Paid: **Date:**
Balance Due: **Due Date:**

Make sure you attach your signed contract with all the stipulations, specifics, and terms of agreement to this worksheet. Be sure to review the tips and questions to ask carefully before signing a contract.

Delegating Ceremony Duties

Set-Up & Decoration Crew

These people help with any additional decorations that aren't done by the florist or site coordinator.

Name:
Contact Number:
Name:
Contact Number:

Miscellaneous Ceremony Delegation

Duties:
Name:
Contact Number:

Duties:
Name:
Contact Number:

Duties:
Name:
Contact Number:

Duties:
Name:
Contact Number:

Duties:
Name:
Contact Number:

Delegating Reception Duties

Guest Book Attendants/Gift Table Attendants

Serve as host or hostess who welcome guests, invite them to have refreshments and/or answer other questions. (Refer to Delegating Ceremony Duties Sheet for names).

Master of The Ceremony/Emcee:

Orchestrates the program part of the reception. Announces bridal party, first dance, slide show, cake cutting, etc.
Musicians can also serve as the program emcee.

Name:
Contact Number:
Name:
Contact Number:

Photographer/Fllorist helper

(Refer to Delegating Ceremony Duties Sheet for names)

Gift Person:

(Refer to Delegating Ceremony Duties Sheet for names)

Reception Decorations Crew

These people will help with additional decorations that aren't done by the florist or site coordinators. Duties can include placing favors and centerpieces on tables, decorating head table, chairs, etc.

Name:
Contact Number:
Name:
Contact Number:

Rental Equipment

This person is in charge of anything that was rented from an outside vendor and needs to be collected and returned. Items can include cake knives, cake pillars, lights, tiki torches, etc. Many rental companies will deliver and pick up rented items unless they are small in size or amout.

Name:
Contact Number:
Name:
Contact Number:

Delegating Reception Duties

Clean-Up:

These people help with any breakdown and clean-up needed. They're more crucial in outdoor weddings or weddings held without banquet help. They need to be the last to leave and be aware of any terms of clean-up agreement you have with your place of reception.

Name:
Contact Number:
Name:
Contact Number:

Miscellaneous Ceremony Delegation

Duties:
Name:
Contact Number:

Duties:
Name:
Contact Number:

Duties:
Name:
Contact Number:

Duties:
Name:
Contact Number:

Duties:
Name:
Contact Number:

Here's how brides, grooms, and their families and friends traditionally split up expenses.

Bride and/or Bride's Family

Engagement party
Wedding Consultant's fee
Bridal gown, veil, and accessories
Wedding stationery, calligraphy, and postage
Wedding gift for the bridal couple
Groom's wedding ring
Groom's gift
Bridesmaids' gifts
Photography
Videography
Guest book
Ceremony
Flowers
Music
Equipment rental
Transportation (limo)

Groom and/or Groom's Family

Rehearsal dinner
Bride's gift
Bride's wedding ring
Bride's bouquet
Mother's corsages/leis
Boutonnieres
Officiant's fee
Marriage license
Honeymoon expenses

Attendants

Own attire (bridesmaids' dresses, tuxedos)
Bridal Shower (maid of honor/bridesmaids)
Bachelor party (best man/groomsmen)
Travel arrangements/accommodations

Vendor Contact & Payment Sheet

Type	Name	Phone	Contract Date	Deposit	Balance Due	Due Date	Paid
Alterations/Seamstress:							
Bridal Salon:							
Bakery/Cakes							
Bartending Services:							
Calligrapher:							
Caterer:							
Centerpieces:							
Ceremony Musicians:							
Ceremony Site:							
Consultant/Planner:							
Decorations:							
Equipment Rentals:							
Favors:							
Florist:							
Gift Table Attendant:							
Gift Suppliers:							
Ice Sculpture:							
Officiant:							
Photographer:							
Reception Site:							

Reception Musicians:							
Reception Entertainment;							
Rehearsal Dinner:							
Tuhedo Rental:							
Transportation:							
Travel Agent:							
Tsuru/Crane							
Videographer:							
Other:							
Other:							

Reception Information Sheet

Reception

Site:
Contact: Phone: Fax:
Address:
Website: Email Address:
Name of Room Area:
Room/Area Capacity: Date Confirmed:
Reception Start Time: End Time:
Head Count by: Final Head Count:
Cocktail/Pupus Time: Meal Time:
Color of Linens: Color of Napkins:
Special Instructions:

Total Cost:
Deposit Amount: Date of Deposit:
Balance Due: Balance Due Date:

Service Includes: (Servers, Bartenders, Valet Parking, Set-up, Clean-up, Meal, etc.)

_____

_____

_____

_____

Equipment/Supplies Included in Cost (Tables, Chairs, Linens, Decorations, etc.)

_____

_____

_____

_____

Other Information:

_____

_____

_____

_____

Attire

Bridal Gown	Budget	Actual	Comments
Headpiece/Veil			
Jewerly			
Undergarments			
Stocking			
Shoes			
Alterations			
Garter			
Other			

Bridesmaids	Budget	Actual	Comments
Bridesmaids' Dresses			
Headpiece			
Jewerly			
Shoes			
Alterations			
Other			

Groom	Budget	Actual	Comments
Formal Wear Rental			
Shoes			
Other			
Other			

Groomsmen	Budget	Actual	Comments
Formal Wear Rental			
Shoes			
Other			
Other			

Flower Girl	Budget	Actual	Comments
Dress			
Other			

Ring Bearer	Budget	Actual	Comments
General Attire			
Other			
Subtotal #1			

Misscellaneous

Beaty	Budget	Actual	Comments
Hair/Makeup/Artist			
Manicures			
Pedicures			
Spa Services			
Massage			
Other			
Subtotal #2			

Beaty	Budget	Actual	Comments
Wedding Cake			
Cake Delivery/Set-up			
Cake Topper			
Cake Knife			
Sheet Cake			
Other			
Subtotal #3			

Ceremony/Reception	Budget	Actual	Comments
Site Fee			
Ring Bearer Pillow			
Chairs			

Archway			
Pupus/Hors D'Oeuvres			
Main Meaal/Caterer			
Beverages			
Bartending			
Bar Set-up Fee			
Corcage Fee			
Pouring Service			
Gratuity			
Parking Fees			
Other			
Other			
Subtotal #4			

Consultant/Planner	Budget	Actual	Comments
Consultant Fee			
Other			
Subtotal #5			

Entertainment	Budget	Actual	Comments
Ceremony Music			
Pre-Reception Music			

Reception Music			
DJ			
Emcee			
Sound System			
Other			
Other			
Subtotal #6			
Equipment Rental	**Budget**	**Actual**	**Comments**
Tent/Canopy			
Tables			
Lighting			
Set-up/Breakdown			
Delivery			
Dance Floor			
Linens			
Beverage Items			
Serviceware			
Tableware			
Other			
Other			
Other			
Subtotal #7			

Flowers & Decorations	Budget	Actual	Comments
Ceremony Flowers			
Reception Flowers			
Centerpieces			
Favors			
Gift Table			
Flower Girl Basket			
Delivery/Set-up (Florist)			
Delivery/Set-up (Centerpieces/Favors)			
Balloons			
Candles			
Other			
Other			
Subtotal #8			

Invitations/Stationery	Budget	Actual	Comments
Invitations			
Response Cards			
Reception Cards			
Ceremony Programms			

Announcement			
Save-the-Date Cards			
Postage			
Calligrapher			
Parer Napkins			
Matchbooks			
Wedding Certificate			
Other			
Other			
Subtotal #9			

Transportation	Budget	Actual	Comments
Limousine			
Tip			
Other			
Other			
Subtotal #10			

Officiant	Budget	Actual	Comments
Officiant Service			
Gratuity			
Other			
Other			
Subtotal #11			

Photographer	Budget	Actual	Comments
Engagement/ Announcement Photo			
Formal Bride Portrait			
Wedding Package			
Negatives			
Additional Prints			
Travel Fee			
Enlargements			
Touch-ups/ Chrome Work			
Digital CD			
Other			
Other			
Subtotal #12			

Videographer	Budget	Actual	Comments
Vedding Date Video			
Extra Tipes			
Photo Montage			
Other			
Subtotal #13			

Specialty Products	Budget	Actual	Comments
Bride's Gift			
Webpage			
Groom's Gift			
Bridesmaids' Gifts			
Groomsmens' Gifts			
Rehearsal Dinner			
Marriage License			
Bridal Gown Preservation			
Name Change Fees			
Honeymoon			
Crane/Tsurus Design			
Other			
Other			
Subtotal #14			

Honeymoon	Budget	Actual	Comments
Airline Tickets			
Car Rental			
Cruise Tickets			
Hotel			
Meals			
Entertainment			
Shopping			
Travel Insurance			
Taxes/Surcharges			
Tips			
Passport Fees			
Other			
Other			
Subtotal #15			

Miscellaneous	Budget	Actual	Comments
Subtotal #16			

Total

Miscellaneous	Budget	Actual	Comments
Subtotal 1-5			
Subtotal 6-11			
Subtotal 12-16			
Total			
Grand Total			

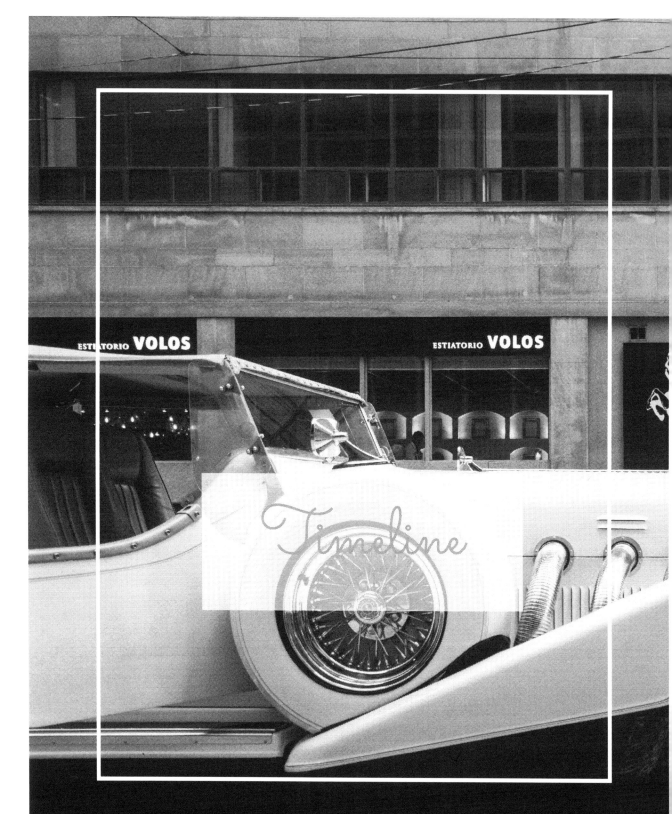

This is a standard timeline. It's written on the presumption that you have nine to twelve months to plan your wedding. There will be those who start planning several years earlier while still others may only have several months. Use this timeline as your list of things to do within the time that you have.

NINE TO TWELVE MONTHS BEFORE

- Announce your engagement.
- Create a preliminary budget.
- Start a guest wish list to help you gauge how many people you will be inviting.
- Hire a wedding planner (if you think you need one). If you're not hiring a planner, select and recruit some family and friends to help you with the wedding planning process.
- Select a wedding date and time.
- Determine what type of wedding you want (size, formality, style, color scheme, etc).
- Select and secure your ceremony location.
- Select and secure your reception location.
- Start shopping for your engagement rings/bands.
- Select and secure your officiant.
- Begin to select and secure your major vendors (photographer, florist, baker, videographer, caterer, DJ or band, entertainment, etc).
- Go to wedding expos and related events for ideas.
- Select, contact, and confirm bridal party (bridesmaids, groomsmen, ushers, flower girl, and ring bearer).
- Select and purchase your wedding gown.
- Mail "save the date" cards to out-of-town guests.

SIX TO NINE MONTHS BEFORE

Narrow down the guest list (ask your families to do the same). Start compiling current addresses and contact information.

Shop for the wedding accessories (headpiece, veil, shoes, etc).

Start planning the honeymoon.

Register with a bridal gift registry.

Select and order bridesmaids' dresses.

Begin planning your wedding day itinerary and reception program.

Begin compiling a contact sheet with names and numbers of all your key vendors.

FOUR TO SIX MONTHS BEFORE

Select and order the invitations and stationery. Prepare all maps and directions for the ceremony, reception, and rehearsal dinner.

Complete the guest lists with up-to-date addresses and contact information.

Begin addressing invitations/announcements.

Remind mothers to start shopping for their dresses.

Select and order the men's attire.

Finalize honeymoon details and make necessary reservations. Apply for or update passports and other necessary travel documentation.

Assign and confirm wedding responsibilities (coordinator or trouble shooter, reception table, someone to handle passing out the leis and flowers to family and friends, ushers).

Select your tsuru design and begin making your cranes.

Select wedding music and review with musicians and/o

Wedding dress fitting.

TWO TO FOUR MONTHS BEFORE

Shop around for transportation companies. Book one.

Confirm the menu and catering details with your caterer.

Buy or create your own wedding guest book (preferably with removable pages for a quick check-in procedure. Some reception sites will provide one if you're spending x amount of dollars).

Set the dates and times with the officiant and ceremony site coordinator for the rehearsal.

Determine your resources for designing and printing the program for the ceremony.

Finalize the florist details, photographer, videographer, musicians, transportation, baker, caterer, hair and makeup, etc.

Make reservations for rehearsal dinner time and place.

Confirm the wedding cake details with the baker and florist if necessary.

Go to pre-marital counseling with your officiant, pastor, or clergy person.

Select gifts for all your attendants.

Hire the limousine or other forms of transportation for the wedding.

SIX TO EIGHT WEEKS BEFORE

Decide on wedding vows. (You can write them yourselves, use standard ones from your officiant, or go to the bookstore or library and purchase a book on vows).

Mail out invitations and announcements.

Purchase, borrow, or make wedding accessories such as the ring pillow, flower girl basket, garter, candles, toasting glasses, favors, centerpieces, card box, etc.

Wedding dress fitting.

FOUR TO SIX WEEKS BEFORE

Estimate expected number of guests.

Buy a gift for the groom or bride. (Whichever applies to you)

Pick up your wedding rings.

Plan the seating for the reception as well as other details for the ceremony and reception. Start writing placards if applicable.

Make sure all bridesmaids have been fitted.

Create a script or outline for your emcee.

TWO WEEKS BEFORE

Make preliminary table assignments if applicable.

Make arrangements for someone to be in charge of collecting and safekeeping gifts after guest check-in is complete.

Handle business and legal details such as name changes, address changes, etc.

Make sure all clothing and accessories for you and the bridal party are ready (veil, shoes, jewelry, etc.)

Call any guests who have not responded yet.

Final wedding dress fitting.

ONE WEEKS BEFORE

Confirm EVERYTHING! (florists, photographer, videographer, officiant, baker, caterer, emcee, entertainment, transportation, ushers, musicians, guest table attendants, ceremony and reception sites).

Give final count to banquet hall or caterer, finalize seating arrangements.

Review any seating details with the ushers and reception table attendants.

Finalize seating arrangements.

Reconfirm your honeymoon reservations. Ensure you have any necessary plane tickets, travel documents, and travel insurance.

Finalize all place cards for reception.

Review all the final details with your photographer, videographer, etc.

Review timeline with your wedding coordinator and/or those assisting at the ceremony and reception.

Finalize your rehearsal dinner arrangements or other plans.

Meet with coordinator or your point person and equip them with any and all emergency phone numbers for all suppliers and vendors. If they are not a wedding planner by trade give them a 3-ring binder with copies of all your wedding day contracts, contact names and numbers, list of those attending rehearsal and/or dinner, copies of the wedding day itinerary to give to all vendors, copy of officiants timeline, flower list, copy of the vows, and everything else they might need to ensure your day runs flawlessly.

Pack for honeymoon or wedding day if you're staying at a hotel or somewhere other than home prior to or following your wedding

Create a wedding day "emergency kit," including mini sewing kit, extra nylons, hairspray, stain remover wipes, etc.

ONE TO TWO DAYS BEFORE

Finalize script or outline for your emcee and go over it with him/her.

Get a manicure or massage.

Review and rehearse all details with your bridal party.

Make sure groomsmen pick up AND try on tuxes or formal wear.

Confirm last minute details with hair and makeup person.

Make envelopes with vendor names with cash payments for services needed on wedding day (limo, florist, musicians, etc).

Have rehearsal and rehearsal dinner.

Make final seating arrangements/guest list. Make multiple print outs for coordinator and guest table attendants.

Create and distribute final contact sheet with all key people/vendor names and phone numbers, preferably cell phone numbers.

THE BIG DAY

Eat something and make sure you drink lots of water.

Allow yourself plenty of time to get dressed.

Prepare for your hairdresser and makeup appointments.

Give your coordinator or point person the tips or final payments in sealed, labeled envelopes to give to your vendors.

Give your marriage license to the officiant.

Start on time. Relax!

Enjoy EVERY second.

Let your coordinator or point person stress now!!

Sample Itenerary

Time	Pre-Ceremony Activities
11:00 a.m.-3:15 p.m.	Girls @ hotel for hair and makeup (Have appts. scheduled and staggered)
1:15 p.m.	XX bringing centerpieces and favors
	XX and XX bringing guest table
	XX and XX will man guest table after ceremony
	XX and XX to help set up rose petal sachets in basket at the entrance
	XX making, bringing, and setting up signs
1:30 p.m.	Guys arrive at chapel, get dressed, and get ready to take photos
2:00 p.m.	Florist drops off flowers at chapel
	XX and XX bring flowers and leis for family and out-of-town guests
2:30 p.m.	XX sets up sound system (small amp, mic for soloist, and lavaliere for pastor)
3:00-3:30 p.m.	Guys take pictures (groomsmen, ring bearer, father of the groom, etc.)
3:20 p.m.	Limo picks up girls from hotel and takes them to chapel
3:30 p.m.	Guys head back to guy's waiting room to hang out, freshen up, and wait for ceremony to start
	XX to set up unity candle (candles, lighters, hurricane lamps, etc.)
3:45 p.m.	Girls arrive at chapel. Go to girls' waiting room to freshen up for pics
	Make sure best man has marriage license and rings

4:00 p.m.	Guest table attendants arrive and set up table
	XX and XX ready to give flowers/leis to family and other assigned guests
	XX arrives and sets up signs
4:00-4:30 p.m.	Girls take pictures (bridal party, flower girl, mother of the bride, etc.)
4:15 p.m.	Guest table attendants ready to check in guests
4:30 p.m.	Girls go back to waiting room to freshen up and get ready to walk out
	Ushers ready to seat guests
	Prelude music begins
	Guests begin arriving, checking in, and being seated

	Ceremony Begins
5:00 p.m.	Processional music starts (Queue song:_____)
	Grandparents of groom seated
	Grandparents of bride seated
	Parents of groom seated
	Mother of bride seated (XX to seat her)
	Officiant and groomsmen walk to altar
5:04 p.m.	Bridal party music begins
	Bridal party enters (List names in order of walking)
	Flower girl and ring bearer walk
5:06 p.m.	Everyone rise for the bride
	Bride and father begin walk (Queue song:_____)
Ceremony Outline (Sample Only)	
	Giving away of the bride
	Welcome and prayer
	Readings (List them)
	Wedding homily
	Vows to each other
	Marriage vows
	Giving of rings
	Prayer for each other

	Communion (Queue song:_____)
	Unity candle (Queue song:_____)
	Pronouncement
	Prayer of dedication
	Presentation and blessing
	Recessional (Queue song:_____)
	Sign marriage license

Post-Ceremony Activities	
5:25 p.m.	Pupus/open bar outside ballroom
	Reception table attendants back to table for check-in
	XX will store gifts in hospitality room and be in charge of locking up
	Gue sts continue check-in and seating
5:30-6:00 p.m.	Pictures with bridal party and family

	Reception Begins
5:45 p.m.	Ballroom opens
6:10 p.m.	Ask people to be seated
	Bridal party freshens up and gets ready to be introduced
6:15 p.m.	Emcee announces bridal party entrance
	Introduce bridal party (list names in order of introduction)
	(Queue song:_____)
	Introduce Mr. & Mrs. XX
	Everyone seated
	Emcee goes over housekeeping (bathroom location, food and drink procedure, etc.)
6:25 p.m.	Prayer for food
	Tables dismissed by banquet captain
	Head table, bridal party to be served
	Queue dinner music (band, entertainer, DJ or CD)
7:05 p.m.	Program begins
	Family introductions (list names in order of introduction)
	Toast by father of the groom

	Toast by father of the bride
	Introduction of out-of-town guests and special guests
7:15 p.m.	Program (bridal party speeches, slide show, special performances, hula)
	Other toasts (bonzai, best man, etc.)
7:40 p.m.	Cake cutting (Queue song: _____)
	Bouquet toss or presentation (Queue song: _____)
	Garter toss (Queue song: _____)
7:50 p.m.	Slideshow
8:05 p.m.	Centerpiece giveaway
	Thank yous
	First dance (Queue song: _____)
	Dance with father/bride and mother/groom (Queue song: _____)
	Money dance (optional)
	Mr. & Mrs. XX visit with the guests
	Open up the dance floor for everyone

| 10:00 p.m. | Limo picks up bride and groom and takes them to honeymoon suite |

And They live happily ever after...

Note

Made in the USA
Coppell, TX
05 February 2021

49795931R00079